ALCHEMY

poems by

Kris Whorton

Finishing Line Press
Georgetown, Kentucky

ALCHEMY

For Randy

Copyright © 2023 by Kris Whorton
ISBN 979-8-88838-329-2 First Edition
All rights reserved under International and Pan-American Copyright Conventions. No part of this book may be reproduced in any manner whatsoever without written permission from the publisher, except in the case of brief quotations embodied in critical articles and reviews.

ACKNOWLEDGMENTS

Thanks to the following publications for publishing these poems.
American Writers Review. "After All."
American Writers Review. "On to Grand Isle."
American Writers Review. "Woman Reunited with Uterus."
The Dillydoun Review. "Even If."
The Greensboro Review #109. "See My Body."
The Thing Itself. "I Took the Desert's Pulse."
Sad Girls Club. "Primrose Path."
Salmon Creek Journal. "How Surgeons Learned to Operate on Beating Hearts."
Salmon Creek Journal. "Alchemy."
Wild Roof Journal. "Early Monday Morning."

Publisher: Leah Huete de Maines
Editor: Christen Kincaid
Cover Art: William Myles Freeman
Author Photo: Sarah Buckner
Cover Design: Elizabeth Maines McCleavy

Order online: www.finishinglinepress.com
 also available on amazon.com

Author inquiries and mail orders:
Finishing Line Press
P. O. Box 1626
Georgetown, Kentucky 40324
U. S. A.

Table of Contents

PART 1.

See My Body 1
A Red Line 2
Primrose Path 3
Even If 4
How Surgeons Learned to Operate on Beating Hearts 5
Below the Sky 6
Mistake #42 7
Postcard to my Spine 8
At Falassarna 9
A Friday in July 10
On to Grand Isle 11
In February 12
Shapeshifter 14
So Careful 15
Peel 16
Outside Mexican Hat, Utah 17
Dark, Now Bright 18
Woman Reunited with Uterus 19
At the End 20

PART 2.

Alchemy 23
Photograph: Baby Comes Home, November 1968 25
Troutfishing 26
On December Days 27
Metal Edge 28
The Monk: Boulder, Colorado 1975 29
You Were a Hurricane 30
The Last Summer 31

Shape of Things to Come...33
I Took the Desert's Pulse 34
For the Life that Ends..35
Haze..36
Don't Feed the Black Bears...37
Home..38
You Said 39
Pause Between...41
In the Morning..42

PART 3.

Unfurling...45
Ocean View with Dogs 46
Re-articulation..47
Work of Art 48
At Home in Water, on Sand 49
What is Rabbit Food?...50
Somewhere Between Highways ZZ and P..................................51
After All 52
Three Bears in Elk Meadow 53
Rafting on the Green..55
Face First..56
See Through Patagonia 58
When You Return 59
Rules of Weather...60
Beltany Stone Circle, Northern Ireland.......................................61
Early Monday Morning 62
Appreciation..63

Part 1

See My Body

My chiropractor displays an x-ray of a neck and I ask him
if it's mine. He says it's a 75-year-old woman's. *So mine*

looks better, I offer. He assures me I am wrong and puts
my spine up. I think mountain range, linked rock formations—

strong and elegant. *You're a mess*, he says as he taps it.
As a child, *mess* meant forty stitches in my cheek,

a flock of geese flying north, and another ten in my forehead,
hidden by bangs, although no one said that word to me

because I was only three. Then mess meant cuts and scrapes
on my knees, shins, elbows, and my dad said it, and that someday

I would be sorry I wasn't more careful, which I knew even then
meant more feminine. More like a snake willing to bend. But how

could I be in a neighborhood of boys, with two brothers
of my own, and a need to be special, somehow. How could I be

when my dad took us fishing, and stargazing, cross-country
skiing, and my mother sent us away to play until dark.

How could I be when I learned to protect myself
by hurting someone else, when boyfriends wanted girls

who were easy, curvy, the Amazon River, and instead
they got me with my blade sharp tongue, barely an indent

between less than a handful breasts and my knees,
and a Saharan need they couldn't fill because I wouldn't

let them. When too many falls and miles running
made my neck and spine a rock-littered, dry riverbed,

the scars on nearly every inch of sun-scoured flesh
became a galaxy, limitless, unknowable, breathtaking.

A Red Line

A red line five inches long runs from the left side of my bellybutton
    to my pubic line. Crooked and tender, it rolls and shifts against

my waistband, like a snake moving away from me fast. When I lean
    into the counter, belly first, when I press with fingertips,

when my dogs jump against me, a current. When my husband touches
    me, a tiny shock in every cell. Abdominal muscles ripped apart,

the surgeon told me, heal more strongly when torn instead of cut;
    my guts moved aside so the surgeons could put titanium in my spine.

Screw me back together. The hospital, a timeless void. In the days following
    the surgery, I was upside down at home. Missing the before, the grinding

of bone, pinch of nerve. The known. I slept in a different bed, guarded
    my center from danger as I learned to walk among rocks in my yard,

a world with six-feet delineations, a Jupiter with pastel-colored
    stripes, not the red, brown, yellow, and white clouds from before.

Primrose Path

Call me Ishmael, my professor read aloud, and I looked
over his shoulder, out the window at a young man who looked
good enough to take to bed. I was like that in those days,

and didn't care about the men I slept with or remember
whether I read a single play in the Shakespeare class
I also took that summer. I thought my Melville professor

was a chainsaw and I didn't understand him.
Moby Dick was filled with too many chapters that asked
questions but never answered them. I was strident, impatient,

and never in love with anyone. Mysteries were secrets
I didn't like. I told my lovers to live with it to quit calling.
Call me Michael, Scott, Ian, Tom, John they said

until I used them up then cast them aside
like the unwanted parts of a whale's carcass,
like Desdemona and Ophelia, who I remember well.

Even If

In my clavicle, I carry a Barbie and her friend's lunchbox,
and an envelope of cocaine a lover gave me in 1984.

I had a heart-shaped stone as well, carved from Lapis lazuli,
but the surgeon removed it along with a tendon he said

I wouldn't need. Sometimes my heartache isn't enough,
so I've added more as I've travelled the world,

from humans who weren't using their angst
and from dead trees. A handful from an amphora I found

in a village on Crete, and another I found on a mountain
top in southern Argentina, a stone's throw from Chile.

In my pocket, I carry all the nights of my life,
over twenty thousand of them now, a number that fills

me with a dread not unlike a hot rash that appears
first on my feet, blistering and turning my skin purple,

before jumping to my abdomen, my forearms,
my neck. I won't survive another twenty thousand

which is another kind of dread. Utter darkness keeps
stealing my life. I can't hold myself still and feel

my way through the wall of tar even if I tell myself
it is only a waterfall and there is another side. Even if

I will find the moon one day. Even if bumblebees
throw gold from their hives. I will count backwards

from twenty thousand until I reach that moon.

How Surgeons Learned to Operate on Beating Hearts

BBC article, July 13, 2020

My husband's story about his aunt freezing her goldfish,
then putting them, thawed and alive, back in the bowl

    after her trip, seems fantastic. His family is prone to tall tales,
so he comes by it honestly. Freezing water works on humans

    too, especially in 1952 for the seven-year-old with the hole
in her heart. Surgeons dropped her body temperature and six

    minutes later, fixed her good as new. An immature cardinal
collides with my French door. While he's stunned and still,

    I crouch close to see the rise and fall, scoop him out of the sun,
place him on a bed of sedum so he can come to. Days ago,

    my friend texted that her mother died, suddenly, hours earlier.
I didn't ask how, only what I could do for her as I thought

    of freezing water, gentle hands and knew it was far too late
for that. My own heart contracts and expands in the shadow

    of death, my father's silences, my mother's warm attention.
How will they end? I wait for the call, yearn to live closer,

    but with my surgery only weeks old, the world of flying
and hugging absent, it is the five-inch incision burning

    at my touch, flinching at my husband's claim he can barely
see the scar, keeping me still. The surgeon tells me my blood

beats 45 times per minute so they had to reset their machine.
He says I bled little, lost nothing. He tells me to live.

Below the Sky

At ten thousand feet, shifting
from one leg to the next, I pull
the unforgiving fabric over first
one boot then the other.

The chill air grips my skin
with the urgency of a lover
as we stand in a green basin
below a great mass of snow

glittering, steadily, sharply
toward the sky even as it melts
ever closer to us. I stand,
half-naked, giddy, exposed

to the sun, the alpine breeze,
your eyes alone. I could almost
forget my other life—
my married life—almost, as I lie

on a bed of damp moss
and feel the press of your warmth.
Snowmelt trickles through
ancient stones, lulling as Lethe.

Mistake #42

I should have said no when you said,
We should get married, but I looked
at the fire crackling, the black
sky pinpricked by too many stars to pick
even one constellation, and couldn't think
how to say I didn't want
couldn't believe it would work.
You would think I loved you only
enough to fill a mountain lake.

I should have said I feared
marriage more than falling.

I should have said
I couldn't be monogamous.
You were gone too much, and I
didn't know how to be alone,
how not to have a man
to pull into my quicksand need.

I should have said no to the men
along the way—
an old friend from high school, lovers
from college, a few men I worked with.
I felt sick of myself, sure I would stop
cheating, but they were M&Ms
and I wanted the whole bag.

I should have said no when
you asked me out at the start. I was in love
with someone else then, or thought I was,
and you, with your river-blue eyes
without a cloud, your easy smile,
one tooth out of line, the way you
looked in my eyes, I couldn't
say no then either.

Postcard to My Spine

I've written to you from this place
before. The space between L5-S1
is not what it was when I was born.

Young. Younger. Before I ran
thousands of miles each year.
Before I fell and ran more. Before

I took that most stressed joint, the spinal
juncture, and exploited it for the fuzzy
intense pleasure pain of running.

Like a relic, a remnant from an ossuary,
I'm not much to look at without
an explanation of where I've been.

I'm nothing without the entry fee, the crowds,
the hope of seeing something new.

At Falassarna

Under the late afternoon sun,
we glide across sand
as diamond shimmery and fine as dust
and spread our towels side by side.

Already in swimsuits, we shed our shirts
settle, bellies down, shoulders
nearly touching. Beyond our shore
sun blinds white, clouds
glow against an impossible blue,
and you study me.

I will not look into your eyes,
you who have brought me to this place,
dangerous, and uncharted,
you, a married man, with black curls
that beg my fingers.
When you say my name, I know
how your lips shape the word that is me,
how I take form in your throat,
on your tongue and slip across your lips.

You lean close, kiss my shoulder,
rest your hand on the small of my back.
Your hot fingertips burn me,
mapping my journey.

A Friday in July

In few hours you will leave.
I sit on your kitchen counter,
legs wrapped around your waist,
arms pulling you closer, burying
my face in your sun-warmed hair.
Your scent, your child inside me.

Already I am two weeks sure
because your heart beats with me
always. You'll go
to the mountains for a month
and never know I hold the center
of the moon.

One day I'll remember your skin
when I smooth clean sheets
on my bed, your eyes in a photo
of a newly calved glacier, your hair
in the coppery glint of a sunset.
I'll meet you on the street and fail
to recognize you.

On to Grand Isle

My husband at home, me no longer living with him
but married still. Divorce papers, signed by me

part of the gulf between us. Another gulf,
3 or 4 states, separate us as does the man

I'm traveling with. After a few hours walking
in New Orleans, we're harried by the too loud,

too stifling, too busy for this weekend
we've cut out of our lives. On a road south

lined by water, marsh grasses
stand bright green against a hazy sky.

Stilt houses rise alone or in pairs on vast
stretches of space and time. The end

of the road a barrier of land between land
sea and more sea. Walkways raised

above sand. Beaches separated from roads
by dune grasses. Birds alight, their cries,

frenzied flight, the only company we seek.

In February

In the jumble of parkas, tights,
two layers of shirts,
we press against each other, hands,

lips searching for flesh
without barriers. The white glare outside
grayed by frozen breath and windshield fog

as heat builds and builds
until we find ourselves
on an unknown tropical island.

No airplanes search for us, no boats,
no other human sound touches
our ragged breathing

as we wonder at our luck in being
lost and hold on and on
until we cannot breathe and must

force the door open. Gasping,
you roll out, planting feet
on snow that groans beneath your boots,

groans again under mine,
not with the pleasure I have been given
but with the pained, sad noise

of bone moving against bone. Bone
pulling apart. A frosty
mountain wind, stiff as a bear's fur

grabs us then lets go. We laugh,
stand without parkas, thrilled, arms thrust out,
while the air first strokes its fingers

through our hair, up and down our spines, bellies
then presses, insistent into our lungs.
Under a sapphire sky

great pines and spruce bow
under the late winter snow,
sparkle in sunlight, beckon me forward.

Your car's back tire rests
on a puddle, iced over, unbroken by our presence.
Such ice can hold the weight of the world.

Shapeshifter

You desperate bird,
you eye me from above, follow me,
each day stealing a little piece of gloss
from a marriage never meant to be:

a glove I left behind with my hand
still a ghost inside the fabric,
an eyelash on your pillow,
the tip of my heart, broken free.

You hop about on the edge of my sight,
a specter, and learn the woman I am the one
who is flattered by your eyes on me.
Cupid. I am desperate for you,

for the touch of your lips and tongue,
for the press of skin to skin.
You burn a wildfire through me,
shape all my thoughts of self into some strange

beast, too fantastic to understand.
Your fingertips stroke heat and wonder
from my bones, until I become something new
and can no longer abide you,

for you are not a god who has lost
your taste for shiny things, one who
can wait for a tornado life to ground itself.
You are a crow unable to say no to anyone.

So Careful

Those men, boys to the core,
my ex-husband worked with

loved practical jokes. Buckets
filled with water perched on top of half-

opened doors. Peppers laced with numbing
agent to lull the man who ate them

into eating far too many. My ex
avoided the jokes, tried

not to laugh, walked the tight rope
of humor at someone else's expense.

He was the youngest of seven, learned to give
one brother the space of the neighborhood,

the fields around their house, no shared
friends, the opposite end of the table

at mealtime, far from the fist, the sneer.
My ex learned to keep his words, his heart,

close. Too close for me to keep him.

Peel

> after Kwame Dawes' "Peach Picking"

I peel back his tender skin,
find his red center in the nest of his ribs,
reach for it, cup it gently
in my hands as I remove it
and place it in a worn cedar box; he
won't need it now that I'm gone.

No more hexes, no more teetering
between the house and the sea.
I'll take his heart, watch him
try to move forward, stiff as a soldier.

He'll say he loves. I'll watch him
place his arm around this woman
or that, but I'll know he is tender,
raw, his skin childish and new,
his ribs an empty cage
for the barely beating muscle
I keep in fresh straw.

Outside Mexican Hat, Utah

      A crow lifted from the roadside. We crossed over
a hill and the land fell away a thousand feet.

      Gravel beneath the wheels. Sky held us
beyond the wall of the truck, beyond

      the two spare feet of road before earth gave way
and there was nothing to keep us there.

      We drove a minute more and I thought I might say
This is it or *I feel alone when I'm with you.*

      Instead, I said your name as a pickup came around
the first of far too many tight curves and struck us in the side.

      You turned into it, saving us.
I surely would have turned the wheels out,

      grabbing the air, sending us over the cliff.
Dropping like a great silent stone.

Dark, Now Bright

    for Randy

As day comes on, the sky throws peachy fingered
flames on the horizon. Hulking mountains to the right,
a hill behind us, we walk the city until mid-afternoon. Fat flakes
drift from a sky the color of polished silver, salt coats our lips, hair.

Storekeepers greet us, *Bless* for Hello, the only word that makes sense
in this vastness. God speaks. Eyes speak where words can't. Time and wind
speak. Winter storms, volcanic heat, lava flows and lava flowing, eruptions
blasting into the sky ripping open earth-black rock. White mountain ranges

crouch, hunkering animal backs under a blue sky almost neon, vast, open,
shocking, or gray and close as a blanket suffocating. In this stark, quiet land
we walk for hours, pass through narrow streets. Past dark we board a bus
search through pitch night for lights which appear and disappear,

a message travelling years to find us. Now here white, now green,
then gone. In a parking lot a hundred miles from the city, thousands
of miles from home, we lose our breath, find wonder
as the Northern sky shifts dark, now bright.

Woman Reunited with Uterus

Some odd things: a goat wearing a necklace, a teacup-carrying
astronaut tethered as he roams outside the shuttle, a dog

driving a limousine through the narrow streets of Lisbon. Odder
still: the man, your doctor, standing in front of your spread legs,

your feet in stirrups, paper towel blanket covering your exposed
parts as he talks about the vaccination, gas prices, how hot it's been

these last weeks. You want to say, *Get on with it already. It's not
like you're interviewing for a job.* He tells you everything looks

normal and you remember 7th grade biology, your teacher showing
the class a fist sized burgundy Bosc pear, holding the fat end

up. *This is your uterus,* he said, and the boys looked at the girls.
The girls felt the future, and past perhaps, of legs spread

in front of men they barely knew and never wanted to open for
in any way. What a mystery life is when you die a little

a thousand ways, day after day, and no one sees you.

At the End

I expect a frisson of skin sparking
skin with the heat and focus
of the sun's white glare on an ant
or a leaf scorched under a magnifying glass.

I hold your hand a second
too long—waiting, wanting
what I think I should feel, the same way

I sniff the air after a rain, and think,
a dog can smell this plus 10,000 times more.
Nose to the air, I sense something pungent
and rich like ancient soil, dark like smoke.

Part 2

Alchemy

In summer I collected odd leaves
furry-bellied from plants whose names
I didn't know. Dry brown seeds

of a plant I called *tobacco* but still
don't know the name.
Rosehip pods which lay

in my palm like rare, rough-cut jewels.
With a pinch of fine dirt
and water from my canteen,

I crushed them on the flat part
of a lichen-covered rock,
and made a brew I used more

than once to conjure storms.
I called cirrus from the east
with solemn incantations,

watched as they raced
across the vast, treeless plains.
With another potion, I pulled cumulus

from secret green valleys to the west.
Elk grazed and disappeared
as my storm built, tumbling

over a sea of white peaks.
My skin smeared
with the dust of my efforts,

the pungent paste
from my own hand, I was caught
by my conjuring.

The small, gray feathers,
smooth stones brought a torrent
I couldn't see my way through.

Photograph: Baby Comes Home, November 1968

In the chill evening air, snow falls beyond
the picture windows. Fat blobs light as light.

Gray sky, flakes lit by the glow inside. The same
brightness in my mother's eyes, stunned deer

in the road. White faced, she's twenty-eight, too
thin, sleepless. The one she holds has a red moon face.

He'll never learn to read beyond first grade level.
Behind her and across the room, the window,

the long couch, my older brother caught in a still
moment only the camera could capture. Grinning

arms wide. And me, close to her, eyes alight,
just three, wanting the snow, our baby,

my mother's warmth, before the baby, on me.

Troutfishing

My father walks ahead, parting waist high grass
with ease, long strides, fingers brushing
the swaying tops with the same gentle pressure
he applies to my fevered brow. I travel
anxiously, trying to keep up, to mirror his grace,
hypnotized by the way he holds
our fishing poles in one hand as he moves
both in this moment and into the next.

He helps me climb a large boulder
by the stream, and we lie side by side,
bellies to moss rock, overlooking the pool
still and deep as a mirror. Finger to his lips,
he smiles, then sits up and threads
a worm on my hook, looping, looping,
guiding yet pushing, gently. Stay here,
he says, softly, as though we conspire
against the sleek, speckled trout.

I will wait here and round them up
while he goes to the other side
and sends them toward me. I know
one worm won't do much with so many fish,
so I will sing or dance for them,
and they will come to me, gladly
for I am a little girl wild to show
what I can do, how grown up I can be.

As he moves away, I drop my hook
and lean over as far as I dare to watch
my line sink, but it is the waver of my own
small face, pale and so high up, that holds me.

December Days

There at one end, my mother's cousin who would bring
three different wives over the years before he came alone.

On one side, our Vietnam vet renter who slept in a chair
in the middle of his room, combat boots laced

up and flak jacket zipped tight. He couldn't leave
the jungle, the death screams, behind. My mother

invited him to dinner, again and again. He loved us,
but missed his family, hated the reminder he was welcome,

but not home. And there my grandmother's
assortment of old ladies. Each white haired and powder

faced, smelling of *Jean Nate* or *Wind Song*, they kept
her company on the sixteen-hour drive she made

from Illinois every year to bake cookies, run up my
dad's electric bill, and fill her trunk with Coors beer

before she headed home at the New Year. In the aftermath
of her mother's visit, my mother nowhere

to be seen, my brothers and me back in school,
the renter ever more unsettled, the cousin

and my grandmother moving closer to death.
All of us moving toward a Christmas entirely different.

Metal Edge

It's slick as you chase your brother
around the swings, the glider.
He's faster, but his laughter pulls you
toward him even as he slips away.

You hear your mother's voice
in your head. *Be careful,* she says. *Take care.*
You understand the words she doesn't say.
There's more out there to hurt you than you know.
Don't be afraid or you'll miss it
all. Don't say No to the chance to run.

She's inside with the baby, so there's
nothing she will say or do to hold you back.
You take the first step. Then another.
And run. Laughing.

You reach out. Grab the edge of his t-shirt. Maybe just.
Then it's out of your fingers and you're falling
forward, cheek to metal, pipe sinking into your skin.

The Monk: Boulder, Colorado 1975

We three, my brothers and me, and our friends had free rein
in the hills behind our house, on those trails, in those woods.
No mother kept us home. We searched for a cave where a monk
had set himself on fire to protest the war. Wanting to find him,

see his burned body, we made sandwiches—PBJ maybe, or baloney
and mustard—hiked the hills, explored the boulders, but didn't
find the cave, even though we went out day after day that summer.
Hot sun, dust dry trails, the smell of hope fading with each day.

By August, school was closing in and we still didn't have a body.
Once, a wasp stung my cheek. We all got poison ivy, scratched
arms and legs, ran out of water, found stones shaped like arrowheads.
But no charred remains. Not the ones I imagined just inside the entry,

a cross-legged man, still recognizable but burned to a crisp. The cave
would be a huge cavern, like a cathedral I saw in pictures, with the smell
of gas and flesh filling the air. One day, we found an almost path that wound
up through dark pines, house-sized boulders. There, some hundred

feet higher, an opening. My older brother went in first, the neighborhood
boys next, then my little brother and me. We were the only bodies
in that too small space. Vietnam was behind us by then. That monk
wanted to be the orange fire of napalm in the jungle. That's what

we heard, though now I can't say where. Monks lived in my small
city. Buddhists prayed in houses near campus. At the Buddhist school.
A man carried a drum, wore red and yellow robes. He walked
to Rocky Flats protesting nuclear power; he walked the streets

for all the days of my childhood. I thought it might be him, burned
in the cave. I hadn't seen him for months or forgot I had. The cave
had rocks, dirt, but no black bones left behind. No ashes. We searched
for scuffs marks, a message, a memory, something besides emptiness.

You Were a Hurricane

You were a hurricane with an enormous eye
where I lived nearly all the time until the storm returned and I
held on tight to whatever was around. I found a letter from you
last night and threw it away before I could be set off course.
The first time I read it, over twenty years ago, I learned
how I'd failed to be an obedient girl.

You were a Mrs. Potatohead with eyes and mouths,
ears and hats that could be changed out by someone
else, but I think you changed them out yourself.
Glossy, wide eyes, the bit of teeth
between your lips. Never a wide grin for me.

You are a stinging nettle with scalloped leaves, veined, a map
I will never learn to read. Covered in hollow, needle-like hairs.
Always pretty, but untouchable. When I get too close,
tell the truth, I cross you and you make me burn.

The Last Summer

    for my mother

From the unlocked and pulled-open door,
the close, musty air poured out of Gramp's
country house like warm molasses kept
in a jar. We stepped back for a moment,

my brothers and I, then filtered in, one by one,
touching doorknob, cracked countertop,
chair back, smooth, oak-topped table, and—
in the same way we had watched you

every time before—we breathed in slowly,
collecting our memories from the dense old
air, damp from rainy winter nights
and long months of thick silence eased

only by the mice living in the kitchen hutch
and nesting in forgotten armchairs
stashed in the corners of rooms.
We left you in the kitchen

as we chose beds, calling "Mine!"
and ran from room to room, our water skipper hands
skimming across the walls. Our eyes barely saw
the age-darkened portraits of faces we never

knew. The whole of outside awaited us while
you unpacked. That first day, we searched
for close-to-home secrets in the closest oak's
hollowed-out center, in the dusty,

broken tools of the corner shed, until we wanted
more, something farther from the sprawling,
faded yellow house. Crossing the yard
through grass that snapped

and bit at our ankles, a forgotten
dull green of a late, dry August, the
maples and oaks seemed to tremble
in the quiet air. Freed from the sight

of the house, from the chance for your voice
to call us back, we ran the old path
through the woods sloping gently, pulling
us along toward the lake, the dock,

to that one point of going out or coming back.
Through a clearing in the trees, the lake lay
below us, almost white, the flat sky
reflected in the quiet waiting water. Each step

brought us closer, until—standing on that dock—
it seemed I had never been there, never seen
that exact white glare, the secret green of water
that always before was blue.

Shape of Things to Come

My mother's navy mini dress,
long mink-brown hair, eyes
doe-like, tear-filled. She leaves us
for her grandmother's funeral.
We are too young to go. Her face
pale. Fat snowflakes dot her shoulders
as she slips into her mother's
Buick. Beyond the exhaust plume,
the driveway is covered white.

She's never talked about this woman who spent
her last years in the state hospital.
Dementia? Alzheimers? I don't know
what they called it in 1966
when she couldn't live at home anymore.
Her mind unremembering
what it should have, holding
tight to what it shouldn't.

When I was an infant,
my mother took me to see her,
and Gram thought I was her granddaughter
as an infant, didn't want to give me
back.

Farthest now from that snow
cold midwestern day, snow cold days
for my family long dead now. Farther
from that place my mother has begged me
not to leave her when she dies.
Instead, I will sprinkle
her ashes in the mountains, Alaska
maybe or Colorado. The home she made
for us. This woman who keeps her stories
close, her past in her throat, overfilling
her eyes. I'll set her free.

I Took the Desert's Pulse

I'm waiting for monsoons in the desert, for earthquakes
and flames, even rowboats long abandoned.
There was once a sea here. A sea is a desert too;

two expanses, both blue, now gray as a storm blows in,
now white as the sun shrieks in the sky. This plain
is sprinkled with tranquility and parched. By day,

scurrying and hiding mark its heart. At sunset,
blood fills the silence, birds rush overhead. I sniff
the air, feel the eyes of a hundred creatures,

rest my palm on the ground in the center
of a circle of rocks left by no one. Someone.
Breathe out. Still. Close my eyes. Still. Listen

with the blackness behind my eyelids, thin air
in my nose, across my skin, beneath my feet.
There, inside the pant and exhale of this crossroads,

a pulse of moisture as strong as Thursday
looking to Friday. I trace it south to Mexico,
feel it bleed, northward, to me.

For the Life That Ends

In the hallways at school
a boy two years younger than me,
my brother's age.
My brother, would never
walk those tile floors.
My brother was Down's Syndrome,
sunshine in my heart. The boy
fished after school, walked along
a busy road by the lake smiling,
whistling. A boy
with a future.
A boy whose life ended
when the driver looked away
at a red-winged blackbird
perched on the barbed wire fence
or glanced down at mail
that slid off the seat when
he turned, or he was looking
at nothing, at everything else,
at the air and the land,
at the road in front of him
but not at the boy just outside
the white line, not at the boy,
fishing pole in hand,
his blonde hair
a shock of yellow
in the sunshine.

Haze

This morning, tornado weather. The sky
a peculiar flat blue. No clouds. No wind.
A stillness not unlike
the careful way you move through
your parents' house now, afraid of the comments.
Masks are a burden. Fauci's a liar.
Gas is too high. Electricity's expensive.
Their world is the worst
it's ever been.

You can't see the cacti on the mountainsides.
Is it smoke haze? *This desertscape is*
burning; we're using all the water. Ruining
our sky. Ourselves. Your world is the worst
it's ever been.

You wake with a headache each morning.
From the pillow, air pressure,
the stress of not saying what you think,
of watching
your parents become theirs,
you become them.

Don't Feed the Black Bears

They glisten in the sunlight, sleep, sometimes belly up,
move back into the woods to their shaded Edens

away from the lines of cars and tourists taking pictures.
Once in Yellowstone, in our Volkswagen van my mom

scratched her cornea on the glovebox door as she searched the floor
for a dropped Jolly Rancher, watermelon, for me, the carsick child

who wished to run alongside the van rather than sit still.
My dad hummed as he drove under that huge Wyoming sky—blue

clear to heaven. In the clinic waiting room next to us
a seated man bent forward, his face the color of old asphalt,

a bloody bandage clasped to his chest like a too early baby.
An hour later, we left with a pirate's patch on my mother's eye.

He lost his thumb to a bear she told my dad, thinking I couldn't hear.
They'll move that bear, he said. I pictured the man, flannel shirt

blood free, holding out a piece of melon, offering a slice of honeyed sun.
Even I knew bears eat thumbs. Don't care about human frailty.

Home

with its western mountain border,
skyscrapers of once sea sand, now stone,

covered with pine, spruce, and crumbled rocks
beneath a sky like a perpetual blue moon.

I long for the cinnamon, raging streams,
the sunlight like a two-faced child, the streets

of ink and Payne's gray. My homeland,
my buzzkill, my roots. My slamming door.

Buddhists, Liberals, dreamers, and frat boys,
all a tsunami of wolves, charmers.

A punk-Lolita of a city. I was happy there, even
when I wasn't, even when it wasn't Manhattan,

not a place of ribbons, parties, and half-sleep.
For me it was always a cocoon, a mud pie,

a hammer. My bliss. My Lazarus. A loud crunch,
daily bread, my inspiration, a sea maiden edging

the Great Plains. How I miss the ambulance
that was home. How I miss the thud, holding

hands, the before and after sex ended,
the crisp air, a canvas, a future. How I miss

blue junipers, chicory, wolf spiders, vistas.
How I miss my pocket full of rosemary and awe.

You Said

I would end up pregnant in high school or in jail.
Maybe you didn't say it, but I felt the collective release of breath
when I graduated. None louder than yours. I might not
have made it without your doubt. My misdeeds and those
done to me scar my flesh, my joints, my marrow
but are as unknown to you as the hours I spent in my room
wishing you were not dead but gone.

You said, *Don't talk back* when I tried to get free of the heavy
way you stilled me. A black cloud. Tight, clipped words
clamped around my wrist. I knew long before you did
I could never be the right girl child.

You said, *A woman needs to be able to change a tire…change her oil…
to not be dependent on a man.* You said to find someone rich and learn
to love them. You said, *You know nothing about this world and how
it works.*

You said I would be sorry I didn't protect my skin from the
high-altitude sun where we lived. You said, *Abuse
doesn't have to be physical or verbal. It can simply be absence.*

You said you knew men better than I did, assured me
they wanted something more than what they said; I didn't care
because I wanted it more.

When I moved abroad, you said, *Stay as long as you can.
We'll send money if you need it. You'll never have this chance
again.* This is what I remember
thirty-five years after it occurs to me
you never said I shouldn't go.

You said you think more about death as you get older and now
you know how close it is. Your own father dead when he was 3 years older
than you are now, and the crack of sadness, jittery fear
in your voice, something I don't want to understand.
I think about death, wonder how your words
Nothing in life is fair made me the person I am.

You said, *This is how you cast a fly rod,*
this is how you clean up after people
who leave trash behind.

You might have said you loved me when I was young.
I don't remember.
But you always held my hand, tight, hold it still
when we see each other. Warmth and smoothness fill me,
sunlight, trout in the shadows, laughter, rare but belly deep,
the sound of thunder outside our tent
as we all slept, safe inside. The way you smile when we talk.

You say, *Go and live your life. I'm glad you didn't listen to me.*

Pause Between

A tape in your drawer is labeled
"Reid's pre-born heartbeat." The ink

is black, the label white,
as though it can be written in words

and understood. I imagine the ultrasound,
the tiny shape in the image—so hard to decipher

if you don't have a doctor telling you
this is the uterine wall, this is the bladder—

and the beat that sounds just like it should
like a new life pumping, gaining strength

in the shelter of its mother. It is this steady
thump thump thump with static

that I hear when I think of you.
Half of that thump is you, the pulse

of a tree growing, the sigh of a bird
between songs, the split second when you run

and have both feet off the ground,
the moment you move in to kiss me

and our lips nearly touch.

In the Morning

we startle a hawk ripping guts
from a chipmunk.
The hawk shrieks once
before flapping off. The guts remain,

draped, glistening.
Life against death, the sun
still low on the horizon on this
new day. On the trail, fresh

from last night's rain, no news
of Ukraine, bodies found
instead of lives, my father's illnesses—
skin cells cut away,

the scalpel a claw,
beak needle sharp, bone marrow
pulled from bone. Above
the hawk waits
as we move on.

Part 3

Unfurling

In the black net of slumbering
home, yard, woods the heater rumors
behind the house, whirring to drown us
in sleep. An owl complains
the chickens are caged for the night.

Beyond the pen, a vermillion fox
blends with fall leaves.
Screams. Pierces the silence.

My chickens pace in their pen
waiting for sunrise
for scratch from my hand.
They'll pick the fat flesh of my fingers
anxious hungry greedy to eat dried corn
and grains. I'll stroke black gold
golden black backs, answer
their clucks murmurs purrs.

The coffee maker
clicks on, its scent
our morning music.
Beyond the wire
green unfurls, an endless
sea-like territory. Uncrossable.

The human eye can see
more shades of green than any
other color. No edge or limit
blurs the known.

Ocean View with Dogs

        The eldest gazes out at navy water,
denim blue sky, bobbing pelicans,
a fury of gulls and terns fishing. With that milky
white cataract hazing one eye and starting
in the other, all is a Rothko painting, *Ocean View
22*.

        The youngest chases sandpipers, black
and white divers she has no wish to catch,
only to scare. Her barks pierce the shush of incoming tides,
her paws throw sand sprays as she breaks to run
into her wild dream.

        The middle boy frets, paces, shifts
on four feet, moans, and woofs at me to throw
a piece of antler-shaped driftwood as I do in our green
Tennessee woods at home. Beyond us the moving
horizon, wild waves at the vanishing point, my view
calm, an emptiness when I look where they aren't.

Re-articulation

        We find a skeleton in the woods
intact, minus hide or muscle, sinew,

        and circle it. The sharpish snout suggests fox,
but maybe my dead dog's bones

        have slipped their tendons, pushed free from earth
as happens with those most loved.

        You say you'll reassemble the bones
using wire to recreate what is no longer there,

        then *Let's go abroad over Christmas.*
Take a backpacking trip. My mouth says words

        even I don't hear. What I want to say is how
do we leave what we can't forget?

        How do we go on with the picked-clean bones?
When there are only spaces, when we lose

        our form, we can never again be whole.

Work of Art

At the Kunstistorische, Vienna

In a second-floor gallery, fretting hands
lifted Christ from the cross and eased him
gently into his mother's arms seconds
before I walked in. Now he is wan,

near death, with angry, oozing wounds.
His followers gather close, look on
with misery. But it is Mary I watch,
wise-eyed, as she searches for a break

in the heavens, finds clouds parted,
and a light shining down with the answer
she seeks, the one that makes her burn,
the one that allows her to accept

this man's death as she accepted his life
into her body. It is this Mary I watch.

At Home in Water, on Sand

Dolphin fins peek from the sea, not content
with the slip of water against sueded skin,
but hungry for the pleasure of rose-
bright light against their indigo world.

We watch from shore, air cooling
around us, dogs crowding our chairs
as though they too feel awe at this daily
affair. How can they not wonder, as we do,

at these lives lived below the surface,
the way these sleek muscled mammals move
between worlds while we, land-bound, lumpy,
impaired, long for their ease underwater.

As a child, I dreamed I was an otter,
a mermaid, a person who could swim. Instead,
more than once I nearly drowned. Water filled
my throat, my lungs, weighted me in the darkness.

But there, in the in between, a stretch of liquid sky,
a sudden lightness to grab life as a sleek and strong human,
one at home in water, on sand, one who floats, basks
in that rose-bright light, knows that indigo sea.

What Is Rabbit Food?

My friend is talking about journaling and diet,
taking control of her life. The things
we can control. I hear "rabbit food."
Kale. Butterhead. Carrots.
Or the processed pellets you can buy.

I had a rabbit when I was a child.
My parents bought her food which smelled
green, earthy, living. Holding her,
ears like silk, like the lamb's ear plant, I wept.
I rub a leaf every time I pass
the reminder in my yard.

My friend says, *Appreciation*? And I can
still feel the weight and warmth, a life I could
keep in my arms, care for without words.
I say, *For something*
we don't want. For the thing
that makes us scared.

It doesn't fill our garden, our plate.
It comes from places we don't expect:
the deep emerald of kale and rabbit food,
the soft fresh green of lettuce,
the surprising crunch of a carrot,
the soft weight and heartbeat of a living
creature, the thumb and forefinger
on a lamb's ears.

Somewhere between Highways ZZ and P

In the kettles and moraines
of southern Wisconsin,
in the banjo strum of the green toad
and the strange, garbled call of a bird
we can't stop to find, in the cycle of our breath,
there is a nowhere land of day and night,
of wanting to sleep so deeply
not even the gods can wake us.
The vibrant day's green
makes my head throb.
The night's black is solid as pain.

The distance we cover
makes us forget the earth we already
crossed over until we step
from the woods onto Highway ZZ,
and the beam from my flashlight
shows a starless, custard-dense sky,
curving trees, the luminescent
stripe on the road. Night moves
to the flat, in-between time.
The birds start up.
You stand like a sleepwalker.
I wish for daylight
to bring you back.

After All

Grace's ashes reside in a thimble-sized container
inside a small, covered trinket dish.
She wanted to be broadcast
in a place she'd never been
or a place she loved. Now
she is tucked away like the tiniest
Matrushka doll. Setting her alight
makes my heart clench.
Some parts will land, others
will find leaf tops, riverbeds. Some will drift
to space. To that place of no sound.
No light between stars and planets.
Vastness too large for my brain.
Sending her into nothingness
scares me.

Ending up as nothingness
scares me. All of my parts alight,
miniscule particles of brain and bone
that could be spread across a glacier.
No body to mourn. No
sure place forever; once a glacier,
a lake, then rain, mist, air.

Instead of cremation, I want to be
the person found in the snowbank, parka
unzipped, eyes closed and face
peaceful. Or better yet, smiling.
There on a mountainside,
Everest say, or somewhere in Antarctica,
Siberia, even Pluto if I could travel all
those miles or lightyears before death
came to me. Before nothing
becomes nothingness
forever.

Three Bears in Elk Meadow

We run, tired to our souls, toward a lake
we will both see for the first time
from our feet instead of a car.
The swing of our arms is now a matter

of gravity, not our own effort,
and even our lungs fill up and empty
on their own, mindless of us.
We are not so much of the earth

as on it, connected and disconnected
by motion and a longing to be still
and simply breathe, but the air
that surrounds us is as thin

as the thread of joy we started with,
climbing the first pass and descending
into snow and rain for miles and hours.
We hold that thread still, just barely,

believing in our lifeless feet
that the mountains will give way
to the hills. Miles later, it comes true
and a great lake glimmers below,

postcard blue. Under a sky so bright
we squint and stumble and run on
through a wide meadow, as elk graze
undisturbed by the red of your shirt,

the smell of soap and sweat on us.
The meadow narrows, funneling us
towards what we hope will be an end.
Instead, in the midst of cool green

so new and fresh, and air so charged
with a wild life we cannot see
but feel and breathe, a mama
and her cubs snuzzle for berries

or grubs, snouts to the ground,
so unconcerned about us
that we ease into their pace and walk
alongside them, twenty feet away.

I hear the rustling of their bodies
against low shrubs, the air they take in
and release, our hearts slowing,
the rumble of their blood in our veins.

Rafting on the Green

On a slate-green snake
winding through a canyon in northern Utah
a bolt of lightning strikes a sage bush,

sending fresh summer scent into the air
seconds before the bush bursts
into flame and rain drops its wet blanket.

Clouds hang, cutouts
in a blinding sky. Heat and wind
so vicious dry scours my skin as I float
through curve after tireless curve.

A baby I never knew was growing
inside me breaks loose and pours out,
blood oil thick. Three days later,

I emerge on a desolate plain, hopeless
and sunburned, my skin sandstone,
my eyes white as bone.

Face First

I lean through the open door of the plane
and am suddenly falling, not jumping
so much as abandoning myself
into a headlong, face first plunge,
into wind that rushes in and grabs me,
roaring, roaring, holding me closer
than I want to be held. As I fall,
strapped to a man I only now realize
I barely know, I fall and fall and fall
and scarcely notice that I am rushing
toward my Earth except for the small
but growing ever-larger mosaic
like a many-colored map or pattern
whose arrangement is as mysterious
as what my future holds.

                        I turn
my head from side to side as if
I will spy some other place to go
besides down, a place I might learn
to read where I have come from,
where I am going. But the wind
won't let me think. There is nothing
to hold on to, not even the man
I'm certain I wouldn't recognize
if we met on the street. I feel no closer
to Earth than I was before jumping
but I know I am closer because the gray
bands of highways and roads are no longer
strands of thread. They are wide and clear
as warning signs. Arcs of sunlight
thrown from the metal of cars and trucks
reach up to me and far above me,
even beyond the plane.

                    As I fall,
I find myself in a sphere of silence
somehow close to the one I should know,
somehow like the one I walk
and breathe in. In this quieter place,
trees become as individual as the houses
they surround, and I am closer
and closer to home, thinking
I understand what comes next.

See Through Patagonia

The map's colors and contours look nothing
like the world I am in,
no more than an inch of iceberg
looks like the rest of it
and the drainage I have decided to follow
simply because it represents down,
and seems so clear, so certain in my hands,
is obscured, chiaroscuro,
a living haze of scrubby legna, its bark
brownish red touched with white.

Feet wet, stumbling on rocks,
slipping on moss
no different than what grows at home,
except that this world of stark
rocky peaks and jewel skies uncut by jet trails
is not home, not a land of red earth
covered with gentle honeysuckle vines,
great hardwoods that block sun and cold,
fresh springs, fresh Spring.

But I am in fall and head toward the out of a living
tunnel of slapping branches
covered with small, serrated leaves, which the light,
pure and sharp from a north-facing sun
shines through, a filter of freshest green,
a dry, damp scent of air and water,
the scratch of dead, unyielding twigs
against my cheek, my jugular, my rib,
against me, my sense of where and who
I am.

When You Return

You will need to declare what you acquired
abroad, but don't say you carry sunlight saturating
thousand-year-old stone buildings you passed each morning
as you walked to the Arno, watched the city awaken.

You will need to declare what you acquired
abroad, but don't say you fell in love twice—
once with a British boy-man. The second time
was an Italian man from Sorrento, he of the crow-black hair
glinting indigo when the sun touched his head.

You will need to declare what you acquired
abroad, an airy, heavenly ciabatta made at a bakery
four miles from your apartment, worth the walk twice
a week, and the panini made at the bakery across
the street. The scent of both breads sent you
spinning, your stomach to wonderland.

You will need to declare what you acquired
abroad, a facility for a language so passionate
that ordering lunch and listening to a museum docent
explain Dante's writing was love made words,
tongue and ears stroked inside out.

You will need to declare what you're bringing
home—a bluebird spirit set free, a heart
that will never be complete, part of it
longing always for that place. Not for home
but for the only world where you ever felt full.

Rules of Weather

Don't run across the beach toward a waterspout,
        no matter how close it seems.
The spout spooling you toward it is the same tether
        pulling the water from the gray, roiling sea
toward the sky. You stumble close to the water's edge,
        arms reaching to grab the rope of water
so many miles away, ready to take you up.

Run across the beach toward a waterspout
        while a policeman calls from the pier,
says, *Ma'am, please go back to your car.*
        Until now you've avoided eye contact,
sat up straight, checked your speed,
        and walked the line knowing wise and unwise
exist in a swirl and you must choose,
        even when you want to spiral out of control.

Beltany Stone Circle, Northern Ireland

A sign for Beltany and we pull in and park
to see the place we didn't plan for, a not often visited stop
and path hugged on one side by rock wall

the other by meadow and, some distance off, sheep.
The wall gives way to shaded walk   then forest
tall bare trunks, some kind of evergreen

dark inside this wood. Beyond the trees   fields
rolling in every direction and rocks
a circle placed some three thousand years ago.

Twenty people my husband's height
could lie head to toe   across the open space.
I walk outside the rocks, step

inside and walk again.   Heart beating   echoing
in my feet. The space of this place a wonder.
No sound reaches us here. Not the soft calls

of sheep, nor tractor, plane, nor crow. Mist light air
like breath on an ice-cold morning   falls away as we circle
the circle, study the stones   their ancient stories

locked inside. Grass and trees, green fields
broken only by tree lines.   Again and again.
Unending. We hold hands   circle again   breathing the space

time held still in the full hole at center. Concentric circles
of silence   surround us from above and around until we hear
a crow's caw, hoarse and ancient   from the dark woods.

Early Monday Morning

I can't stop pointing out the stars. Hours before sunrise,
I'm on my front porch, a deck that faces woods

and darkness. We have no streetlight, no neighbors,
so few homes in this part of town, the stars are a map

I'm still learning to read. Below me, my yard is dense
darkness I can't see into no matter how many times I blink.

Above, the stars form a patchwork, some paths, a sequined
banner of bright, less bright. My boy dog sits at my side

awaiting the answer to some existential question I'm not
aware of, one that is bigger than *Why am I here?* And because

the answer doesn't come I think the question might be
Why are there so many shades of darkness? or *Why do we cry*

when we're happy? I show my boy Orion, recently returned to our sky,
and the dippers, constellations I've known since I was a child.

In Argentina, I searched the stars this same way. White and blue,
yellow pinpricks, arms of the Milky Way reaching

from Chile to the mountains behind me. No dippers,
no knife, no belt, no handle to hold the familiar.

The predawn black, all around and above,
as unknown to me on that mountain as I was in that world.

Had I disappeared—a grain of soil in the midst
of a million others—I might never have been found,

as those unknown stars were gone to me, as we all are, each of us,
day-to-day in this world where we think we know our place,

but we can't always recognize what we're seeing.

Appreciation

I would first like to thank Leah Huete de Maines, my publisher, and Christen Kincaid, my editor, for their support and careful attention to my manuscript.

To the journals that have published my work, your acceptance encouraged me to keep writing.

To my teachers, my colleagues, and my students, Thank you for your excellence, encouragement, and support.

Thanks to Jessica Barksdale, who read this collection more than once, and to Maggie Smith, Stephen Corey, Erica Wright, Rick Jackson, Danielle Hanson, Earl S. Braggs, and Andreana Lefton for your careful reading of these poems and for sharing your insights. Each of you helped me make these poems better.

For the Two Sylvias retreats and your special attention to poems created during the retreats, Thank you Kelli Russell Agodon, Annette Spaulding-Convy, January Gill O'Neil, Diane Seuss, Jennifer K. Sweeney, and Traci Brimhall for providing the nudge, the inspiration, and the encouragement I needed to write many of these poems.

Without my writing groups and friends who keep me writing, no words would ever find their way to the page. To Jessica Barksdale, Julie Roemer, Jenny Neves, Mishele Maron, Andrea Clausen, Sarah Blaser, to Judy Myers and my Round Robin partners, to Dana Shavin, Linda Voychevhoski, Mimi Jones Hedwig, Carrie Meadows, Sybil Baker, Tracye Pool, Linda Frost, and Andreana Lefton, Thank you. You are amazing women, all of you, and your continued focus and excellence inspire and guide me.

I am grateful to my family, the one I was fortunate enough to be born into—Ivan and Sharon Hults, Bud and Tonya Hults, and Michael Hults—and the one I married into—Randal and Betty Whorton, and Stephanie Whorton Bingham and Don Bingham. Not everyone has such gifts in their life.

To Cynthia Fallowfield, Chris and Karen Fason, Alanna Frost, Mindy Haworth, and my community of friends and supporters, Thank you for listening and showing up for me.

To those who inspired these poems, please forgive any misrepresentation. Poetry is often fiction and memory isn't always true.

Without Jessica Barksdale, my mentor, my best pal, my sister, I would be lost. You make my life richer every day.

Finally, I can't imagine how my life would look without my husband, Randy. Thank you forever and always. I am grateful to experience this life with you.

Kris Whorton is originally from Boulder, Colorado. She teaches writing at the University of Tennessee at Chattanooga and served as the assistant director of the Meacham Writers' Workshop. Whorton also teaches teens and adults in the community and works with the incarcerated at Hamilton and Bradley County Jails. Whorton's poems have appeared most recently in *The Greensboro Review #109*, and *Salmon Creek Journal*. Her fiction has been published in *Driftwood Press, Scarlet Leaf Review,* and elsewhere; she was an editor and regular contributor to *Roots Rated,* and her creative nonfiction has been anthologized and featured in *Get Out*. Whorton lives in the woods with her husband and two Australian Shepherds.

www.ingramcontent.com/pod-product-compliance
Lightning Source LLC
Chambersburg PA
CBHW020341170426
43200CB00006B/454